How to Mentor in the Midst of Change

Cheryl Granade Sullivan

Association for Supervision and Curriculum Development
Alexandria, Virginia

Association for Supervision and Curriculum Development
1703 N. Beauregard St. • Alexandria, VA 22311-1714 USA
Telephone: 1-800-933-2723 or 703-578-9600 • Fax: 703-575-5400
Web site: http://www.ascd.org • E-mail: member@ascd.org

Gene R. Carter, *Executive Director*
Michelle Terry, *Associate Executive Director, Program Development*
Nancy Modrak, *Director, Publishing*
John O'Neil, *Director of Acquisitions*
Julie Houtz, *Managing Editor of Books*
Carolyn Pool, *Associate Editor*
Gary Bloom, *Director, Design and Production Services*
Karen Monaco, *Senior Designer*
Tracey A. Smith, *Production Manager*
Dina Murray, *Production Coordinator*
John Franklin, *Production Coordinator*
Valerie Sprague, *Desktop Publisher*

Printed in the United States of America

ASCD member price: $6.95   nonmember price: $8.95

ASCD Stock No.: 611-92015

Library of Congress Cataloging-in-Publication Data

Sullivan, Cheryl Granade.
    How to mentor in the midst of change / Cheryl Granade Sullivan.
        p.   cm.
    Includes bibliographical references (p.   ).
    ISBN 0-87120-191-7 : $6.95
        1. Mentors in education—United States.   2. Teacher orientation—
United States.   3. Teachers—In-service training— United States.
4. School administrators—In-service training—United States.
I. Title.
LB1731.4.S85   1992
371.1'46—dc20   92-7919
                                                                  CIP

03 02 01 00 99   6 5

How to Mentor
in the Midst of Change

Any writing task is a personal endeavor. The preparation of this book on mentoring became, among other things, a time for fond remembrances of mentoring in my own life. Therefore, it is with appreciation and joy that I dedicate this work.

To Helen Tucker
who began teaching me when I was in her 8th grade
English class at South Miami Junior High
and continues to teach me in new ways now

and

in memory of Mary and Marvin Sledd
who changed my life with their wisdom and nurturing.

Introduction

The hue and cry among many educators is that "schools just aren't like they used to be." Yet, as Elliot Eisner (1990) graphically describes, schools are very much like they used to be. The people who come to school, however, are changing rapidly. How can educators meet the challenge of directing schools through rapidly changing times in ways that are healthy for individuals and for institutions? How can schools realize the vision of meeting the needs of an increasingly diverse population of adults and children? How will 21st century school leaders attend to demands for change (restructuring) in ways that yield "good" schools? And finally, how do we attract and retain capable educators?

The responses are as complex as the questions. There are simply no pat answers. One approach to such questions that has gained momentum throughout the United States in the past decade is mentoring. Mentoring may also be the key to developing and recruiting personnel for a variety of positions at the school, district, state, and national levels.

If mentoring is to serve as a viable process in the midst of change, we must focus on how a person can *become* a mentor and *be* a mentor, as opposed to simply *doing* mentoring. Therefore, this book serves not as a cookbook, but as a toolkit. It is designed to provide resources, insights, and descriptions about concepts, approaches, activities, and ideas (and ideals) associated with mentoring. It is a professional package that may be used to strengthen a variety of self-contained mentoring programs or to provide skills needed for reform efforts. Educators may find this toolkit particularly useful as they themselves become mentors and encourage their protégés to be mentors down the road.

The final section, "Making a Plan for Mentoring," enables the reader to design a customized plan of action. It parallels the other sections of the text so that decisions that are made can be pulled into a unified outline of starting points.

Concepts of
Mentoring

Whom do you consider to be your mentor?
What did that person do for you?
In what ways was the relationship special?

*It is the supreme art
of the mentor to awaken
joy in creative expression
and knowledge.*

—*Albert Einstein*

What is mentoring? To offer a standard definition of the term is incompatible with the state of the art in the field. "Mentor roles are markedly ambiguous," concludes Judith Warren Little (1990) after extensive research. Such ambiguity may match the chaos in education perceived by many and the changes documented by all. Mentoring roles may need to be fluid and dependent on context and characters (see Figure 1). As we look at the impact of mentoring on schools, the key question may not be "What is it?" but "What can it be?"

Figure 1
Mentoring Responses

What can mentoring be?	As you become a better mentor . . . How will you be:	

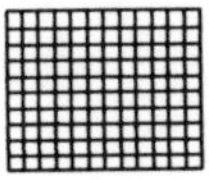

A SCREEN _____ **?**

AN AVENUE _____ **?**

A WISE COUNSELOR _____ **?**

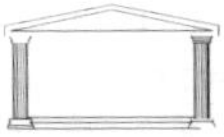

A SUPPORT_____ **?**

A ROLE MODEL_____ **?**

Approaches

When does mentoring seem to "just happen"?
To what extent can mentoring relationships be mandated?
What makes a mentoring relationship work?

> *Life is change, rhythm and*
> *development. To live is to adapt.*
> *Each new situation demands a*
> *giving beyond ourselves and*
> *our habits, which is far from easy.*

—*F. Harry Daniel,* **Letting Go** *(August 1985)*

Recently, educators have begun to view mentoring as a tool for addressing problems of attrition in the pool of the most highly qualified educational personnel. Many formal programs have been developed to focus especially on teachers in the early years of their careers because novice teachers tend to leave education in disproportionate numbers.

Structured mentoring programs often combine the efforts of public schools, higher education faculty members, and state departments of education. Although the formats of these programs vary, a high level of interaction among new teachers, their colleagues, and administrators is a common feature (Jensen 1987). Jensen describes three major models of mentoring programs:

- In one model, the energies of school and higher education personnel are combined. Teacher educators work together with district administrators and classroom teachers to ensure that the transition from student teaching to full-time teaching is smooth.
- Another model emphasizes supervision and coaching from the building administrator or from district staff development personnel. In some cases, the first year of teaching is considered as an internship, featuring intensive feedback from district supervisors.

• A common model of induction features experienced teachers as mentors, who provide the new teacher with legitimate access to a colleague's expertise. The mentor program provides a sounding board for the new teacher's questions and concerns, and mentor teachers may provide formal classroom observations in a format of clinical supervision.

Some states (e.g., Florida, Virginia, and Utah) have mandated mentoring programs to assist teachers as they proceed through assessment/certification processes. In other states, schools or districts have initiated their own efforts. In one design in Douglas County, Georgia, the focus was on professional development of the mentor as well as the protégé (Sullivan and Murray 1988). The Houston Mathematics and Science Improvement Consortium included practicing scientists and mathematicians as mentors to high school science and mathematics teachers.

Though there is a wealth of literature on mentoring among teachers—and for them—less has been generated about mentors for administrators.

Of the models developed for formal administrative mentoring, many have in common the scheme of the planned mentoring program (PMP) designed by Gray (1989). Key components of PMP include:

• Purpose and goal identification
• Identification and matching of mentor with protégé
• Monitoring of the mentoring process
• Evaluation of results and recommendations

Major distinctions occur in formal mentorships in the areas of target groups and mentor criteria. A brief synopsis of varied structured programs, as described by Pence (1989), highlights some of these distinctions, as follows:

1. *Dayton Entry-Year Pilot Program*
Participant Model: All first-year administrators are assigned mentors during their first year of service.

2. *Danforth Foundation*
Participant Model: Mentoring was included in an induction program that involved experienced school administrators and individuals aspiring to become administrators.

3. *Far West Laboratory*
Participant Model: Peer Assisted Leadership (PAL). Practicing administrators assume the role of assessing their own leadership skills, as well as those of their peers.

4. *Oregon Programs*
Participant Models:

David Douglas District—Pairing of new principals with retired principals who were identified as being successful in their years as school administrators.

North Clackamus District—Principals identified as having four successful years in the principalship were paired as mentors with new administrators.

The intent of these formal mentoring approaches is to provide a working knowledge and a building base of skills in effective leadership. Klauss (1981) distinguishes the formal from the informal aspects by asserting:

> The intensity of the formalized mentor relationships may not be as great as that of the informal, highly personalized mentor experiences, but the former nevertheless can have considerable impact on the careers of individuals (p. 9).

At this time, major barriers to effectiveness—in addition to the lack of intensity in personal experiences—come from philosophical differences between the mentor and protégé or between the mentor and school district. These differences have disrupted many productive mentor-protégé programs.

The long tradition of mentoring in fields other than education has been primarily informal. Levinson (1978) observes that "mentoring is defined not in terms of formal rules but in terms of the character of the relationship and the function it serves" (p. 98). One may view the approach as being composed of attraction, action, and effect (Darling-Hammond 1988).

There are no step-by-step procedures to follow as one takes the informal approach to mentoring, but certain aspects are worthy of careful thought. Criteria for establishing mentoring relationships that work include:

- Similar values concerning achievement
- Complementary (not duplicate) factors in skills and knowledge

- Experience in day-to-day requirements on the part of the mentor
- Openness to experimentation with many options (a spirit of seeking answers rather than *the answer*)
- Inclination of the part of each individual to rejoice in the success of the other
- Sense of eagerness for learning and new ideas
- Willingness to listen
- Ability to ask questions

In either anticipating or reflecting on mentoring relationships that are informally established, one should consider several approaches—the *who, what, when,* and *where* of mentoring.

Who?

Because mentoring occurs informally, it generally takes place between two people who share values and aspirations. An established teacher may see potential in another person. An aspiring leader may align with someone already in an administrative role. A traditional pairing in the past has often included an older, established male who sponsors a young, promising male through entry into a career field or into a corporate setting.

Current demographics show dramatic changes in the pool of eligible school leaders and indicate that serious expansion of mentoring must take place. For example, half of all principals are expected to retire within the next decade (Coursen, Mazzarella, Jeffries, and Hadderman 1989). And 71 percent of the current (1990) teaching work force (which often provides administrative talent) is female.

The situation regarding teachers is equally serious. According to the 1988 Metropolitan Life Survey of American Teachers (Louis Harris & Associates 1988) 34 percent of all teachers reported plans to leave the field within five years. Overall, the average age of the teacher work force is increasing; more than half of all teachers have more than fifteen years' experience. Replacements will be needed. General projections for the next decade show increasing numbers of Asian-Americans, African-Americans, and Hispanics in the U.S. population. Current educators will need to push themselves to look beyond candidates of like gender and ethnicity. Mentoring of women and minorities is of high priority and represents a change in the traditional, informal mentoring patterns.

Consider:

■ **For whom would I like to be a mentor?**

■ **Who has already placed me in the role of mentor?**

■ **What are the personal characteristics of the two persons involved that make for a complementary relationship?**

What?

Some of the surface aspects of mentoring approaches can be delineated. They may include orientation, getting-acquainted workshops, and other formal structures. However, highlights from research on mentoring show that successful mentors "take a personal interest in their protégés' careers, share power and expertise, encourage their protégés' ideas, and help them gain self-confidence" (Gray and Gray 1985, p. 39).

The implications are clear: the key to a successful approach to mentoring is to show sincere caring and to foster rapport. Establishing a sense of commitment to the individual and to the relationship may come through discussions, shared projects, or some other joint venture.

Consider:

■ **How can I show that I care about another person?**

■ **Which of the opportunities (projects, discussions) available would be best to share in forging a mentoring relationship?**

■ **How will I avoid filling time with trivial activities that do not provide the foundation for mentoring?**

When and Where?

The logistics of mentoring need to fit with other aspects of personal and professional life. The job must be in sync with the individual and should begin when the mentor is fit mentally, experientially, physically, and emotionally.

The timing question in mentoring is a matter of internal as well as external clocks and calendars. In the largest sense of the question "When?" the mentoring relationship should come at a career time that is right for both people.

In anticipating time factors, it is important that both mentor and protégé protect some on-the-job time for needed dialogue. Some encounters can and should be preplanned, but ad hoc sessions should also be included.

Mentoring is not a staged act that has an unchanging set. It needs one-on-one settings at times—but the relationship and exchanges may also occur in the context of larger meetings and informal gatherings.

Consider:

■ **Where in my current schedule do I need to make adjustments for being a mentor?**

■ **How can my protégé and I indicate that an ad hoc session should take place?**

As you become a better mentor . . .

■ **Which approach will you favor . . .**
        formal?
        informal?

■ **What will you emphasize within your chosen approach?**

Activities

What can educators *do* as mentors?
How does one prepare for mentoring?

> *Those who have torches will*
> *pass them on to others.*
>
> —*Plato*

One of the keys to successful mentoring is the match between (1) what the protégé is, knows, does, and needs and (2) what the mentor provides. The activities included in this section create a compilation of options, not a step-by-step sequence of procedures. Major points are provided to facilitate insights and behaviors for mentoring in a variety of changing circumstances and with many individuals.

Determining Goals

Roland Barth (1988) describes leadership as "making what you believe in happen." Mentoring relationships in schools require definitions of what individuals believe in—what their goals are.

The mentor must hold some personal goals, as must the protégé. Because the individuals are at different points in their careers, the goals will probably differ. Difference is healthy and fine so long as the goals are not in conflict. The mentoring relationship needs to be cooperative, not competitive.

Further, mentor and protégé must share some mutual goals. Perhaps the shared goals will deal with the relationship, perhaps with a particular project, perhaps with implementing change in schools. They may focus on desired improvements in classroom-based instruction or on curriculum redesign. How can goals—individual and mutual—be determined?

■ **State goals using the word** *have*. **If you succeed, what will you** *have*?

■ **Envision an outcome by seeing yourself in the time, place, and activity desired.**

■ **Write a description of yourself, using present-tense verbs—but describing what you** *want* **as opposed to what currently** *does* **exist.**

■ **Sit facing an individual you trust. State your goal using any terms you can. Have the individual repeatedly ask "What else?" until your goal is completely and specifically stated.**

Listening

Look the person in the eye.

Intensely focus on what the person is saying and what is *not* being said.

Stop planning your own comeback—you do not need to calculate your compliment or design your demand.

Take time—don't appear rushed. If you really do have a conflicting agenda, say so and set up a time when you can calmly attend to the protégé.

Energy is required to respond nonverbally, as well as verbally.

Never interrupt.

To listen effectively:

■ **Position the body by leaning slightly forward.**

■ **Consider what the true message really is—verbally and nonverbally. (Some conferencing-skill materials suggest that it is important to consider what is *not* being said, as well as what is said.)**

■ **Remove any physical barriers—try to avoid letting a desk come between you and your protégé.**

■ **Occasionally summarize, using some of the protégé's own words to show that you really are paying attention.**

Building Rapport

Rapport enables two people to agree and disagree with dignity. It stabilizes a relationship so that any event, idea, or conversation becomes only a single occurrence in an ongoing commitment.

Building rapport requires energy but not aggression. It has to be the byproduct of trust, common experiences, shared values, and empathy. Rapport is intellectual and emotional: both head and heart are involved.

Rapport is not a checklist. It cannot be mandated. It emerges as part of a healthy bond between mentor and protégé and accommodates the fluid roles and demands of the fast-paced, ever-changing, and seemingly chaotic environment that characterizes life in and out of school.

In seeking to establish rapport:

■ **Share histories by making personal timelines.**

■ **Work on a short-term, carefully defined program together.**

■ **Decide on a slogan or quote to use as a motto.**

■ **Carefully choose the names by which you call others.**

■ **Discuss ways of handling the most controversial aspects of schooling by working through selected case studies. You might even consider Shulman's (1991) approach of sharing stories.**

Sharing Information and Sources

Information is power. The mentor is almost always—by definition—in a position to be an information broker. To be effective, the mentor must be generous with available facts, figures, interpretations, and sources.

Simply being willing to share information is a major prerequisite. A crucial question then becomes, "How do I provide information to the protégé?"

At this point, all mentors—regardless of job position—need to be good teachers. It is not sufficient simply to tell the protégé in a haphazard fashion what you wish to convey. Look for the protégé's preferred ways of learning and consider carefully how much data should be included at any one time.

To facilitate sharing:

■ **Keep a running list of items to be covered with the protégé.**

■ **Establish regular times for meeting together. Make "keeping up to date" a major priority.**

■ **Introduce the protégé to your sources of information. Consider these sources: formal, informal, human, print, video/audio.**

■ **Write the names of individuals you mention so that the proper spelling is available.**

Laughing and Crying

William Glasser (1986) reminds us that to belong and love is a basic requirement of all humans. To have and express honest feelings of belonging and love requires more than casual conversation or current cliches.

As mentor and protégé share in mentoring, meeting these human needs may come through shared work and common struggles—but the relationship may also be forged as the two individuals laugh and cry together. To share the emotion of the moment or the effect of the experience is truly to share.

Willingness to laugh and cry—that is, to include emotion as a part of the relationship—may help both mentor and protégé keep alive some of their visions about what education can be. It may improve morale and relieve stress as pressure mounts during times of rapid change.

The sharing of humor, joy, tension, or grief may be one of the more difficult aspects of mentoring. There is no formula for making it happen. Some observers may regard time spent laughing or crying together as "off-task" or "unbusinesslike"; but one key to effective schools is the good educator who, by definition, must be a healthy person.

To focus on human emotional needs:

■ **Check yourself each day to determine whether you are keeping you own balance with regard to the emotional aspects of the work.**

■ **Observe others for the forms that "laughing" or "crying" can take.**

■ **Take the lead in sharing humor and sadness with your protégé (i.e., model the behavior).**

Speaking the Native Tongue

If one goes to Australia and says "good morning" or "hello," the locals know the words. However, in order to derive meaning, they must interpret. If, on the other hand, the visitor says, "g'day," the interpretation has been made in advance.

Mentors not only need to use words that protégés recognize; they need to choose language that requires no further interpretation. They need to speak the protégé's native tongue.

In speaking for understanding, mentors should define acronyms (e.g., not all neophytes know that ASCD stands for Association for Supervision and Curriculum Development) and repeat those definitions. When using a nickname, a mentor should at least parenthetically include the formal name by which the protégé may recognize the individual (e.g., if you refer to "Jim," clarify by saying "Dr. James Brown"). If there is a history of multiple names, all names need to be included. (A good example might be the federal programs known as Title I and Chapter 1.)

A different kind of interpretation is required as one considers the age and background of the protégé. Recently, a man approaching 80, who was returning to college, received his school's history award. One of his fellow classmates sighed and complained briefly, "But it was so easy for him—he lived through it all." Such a story is a reminder that personal memories provide a special context. Events that occurred before the protégé's birth or entry into a school or system require more careful explanation than do occurrences within the individual's experience.

To speak the native tongue:

■ **Screen important events in the school or system in relation to the protégé's experiences.**

■ **Create a list of acronyms you frequently use and define them.**

■ **Listen carefully to the protégé so you can use some of that individual's preferred language.**

■ **Check periodically to make sure that the terms you use are understood in the same way by both you and your protégé.**

Challenging for High Achievement

Many bricklayers can lay up to 600 bricks per day. The average number of bricks placed (and paid for) each day is 400. Why, you may ask, do those capable of laying 600 bricks not perform up to their abilities? Observers contend that lack of monetary reward and personal abuse in the form of taunts and threats from fellow workers inhibit productivity. We often see a tendency toward the average in the workplace.

Simultaneously, Americans are inspired toward excellence. Ron Edmonds' (1979) early studies of effective schools pointed to the importance of expectations for high performance in student achievement in schools. Best-selling books have included titles such as *A Passion for Excellence* and *See You at the Top*.

These examples point to the conflicting messages received by aspiring educators. Mentors may need to overtly frame the conflict and invite the protégé to consider personal dilemmas and options regarding quantity and quality of work outcomes.

If the individual's ideals are lofty and include a vision of high performance, then it may be important to define that vision and work backwards from it to set some achievable steps that lead in the chosen direction.

Slogans and mottos often help individuals to be stress resistant and to stay on their chosen tracks. Mentor and protégé may together set a slogan that becomes a "cheer" for high achievement.

Toward excellence and achievement:

■ **List the conflicting (pro and con) messages to administrators regarding excellence.**

■ **Ask the protégé about the quality of work expected of the protégé and others. Be specific—what do various activities or accomplishments look like?**

■ **Choose or coin a slogan or motto that serves to promote high achievement.**

Identifying Strengths and Weaknesses

The most successful people in high leadership positions are able to evaluate their own performance. This kind of self-analysis, if achieved, comes through a variety of experiences.

Mentors can provide evaluative information to protégés who, in the early stages of their careers, may be unable to get clear pictures of their own abilities.

In identifying strengths and weaknesses, mentors need to observe carefully, gather data, review their findings in terms of their own knowledge (including their understanding of research), and conference with protégés to obtain more information and to share perceptions. Sometimes the emerging pattern springs easily from objective data. At other times, understanding the implications of various bits of information may require the creative insight of the mentor.

If the overall pattern of abilities and characteristics shows that the person is not doing well and that the pattern is likely to continue, then part of the mentor's job is to enable the protégé to see that pattern. This does not mean that either person failed, but that the job and protégé do not match.

To facilitate assessment:

■ **Collect a variety of documents that provide items by which to observe protégés.**

■ **Expand the range of conferencing abilities to include:**
—**Listening and other nondirective behavior.**
—**Collegial sharing through brainstorming and discussion.**
—**Directive behavior such as telling. (See Carl Glickman's (1985) work on developmental supervision.)**

■ **Develop a small file of short research summaries about critical educational issues.**

Coaching for Development

Good coaching involves a precise review of specific types of behavior—and general, ongoing cheerleading. Coaches may or may not call the play. But they are knowledgeable about the game—its rules, its strategies, its moves, its personnel—and they are wholeheartedly committed to a winning profile.

The mentor as coach can help protégés maintain and refine those desirable skills and kinds of behavior they have already acquired. Coaching can remediate deficiencies and expose areas of potential weakness.

When effective, coaching focuses on behavior. Feedback must be specific and must be given in amounts and language that makes sense to the protégé. Simply saying "Do better" or "Try harder" is not appropriate coaching.

Parents, teachers, students, and the community should be on the same side. But in today's society, one of the chaotic trends is often to see these groups in adversarial positions. The mentor must be able to analyze and help devise ready responses to the groups when they are attacking. Further, the mentor needs to assist the protégé with both coping in the moment and learning to generate approaches for dealing with such situations.

In coaching:

■ **When the protégé knows, intellectually, what to do, provide encouragement for repeated practice.**

■ **Chart the protégé's progress in an area needing improvement.**

■ **Discuss an area of fine ability, and work with the protégé to increase skill and confidence.**

■ **Provide examples and models—in real life, film, and literature—of desired levels of competency.**

■ **Use steps of a peer coaching program to ensure careful implementation. [See Pam Robbins' (1991) work on implementing a peer coaching program.]**

Providing Appropriate Support

Mentoring is not the protégé's insurance policy: it does not provide a guarantee of success. The job of mentor is to create a context in which the protégé has the opportunity to succeed. (This means that the protégé may succeed—or fail—based on the protégé's abilities and achievements.)

The mentor may provide support by interacting with the protégé regarding skills, insights, or personal needs associated with the job. The mentor may model or directly teach some aspects of the work. And the mentor may provide ongoing or incidental encouragement regarding either a particular task or the general stamina needed to enter the education field and succeed in it.

At times, a mentor may provide appropriate support through activities within the organization of the school, district, or state. The mentor may act to intervene or provide a buffer zone during difficult times. Sometimes the mentor's roles may be invisible to the protégé; at other times, the mentor may be highly evident as one who opens doors or promotes the protégé.

Key issues in providing support include the amount of help to provide, when to intervene, and whether to be visible. Mentors must also decide when to state the limits of their support to protégés and others.

Because mentoring is more personal than procedural, one may attempt to do all the right things as mentor and still have the relationship not work. Sometimes the relationship fails for reasons that will never be understood. If in examining the relationship—the facts, the feelings, and the outcomes—one concludes that the mentoring relationship is unhealthy

---

To provide support:

■ **Determine whether support is needed within the context of the mentoring relationship.**

■ **When providing assistance, offer help in terms of the task and its difficulty (rather than focusing on deficits of the person).**

■ **Focus on an opportunity for success, not guaranteed success.**

■ **Consciously decide what you can and will do and set some points at which you will reevaluate the situation.**

---

for either mentor or protégé or for both, then both participants should generate and actively seek alternatives. It is important to acknowledge that the relationship is not working, but it is unnecessary to analyze all the reasons why.

Recognizing Accomplishments

Fortunately, some things go right for mentors and protégés. Research from the corporate world reinforces the importance of celebrating these accomplishments—even minor ones.

Recognition, when it is offered in a manner that is timely and appropriate to the individual, serves as a reward for past performance and an inspiration for future efforts. Educational institutions—whether schools or systems—generally have organized programs for employee recognition. Such programs must by necessity be normative. Mentors have the opportunity to personalize such expressions to protégés.

On the surface, there appears to be minimal variation between a short note, a spoken "Good work!" and a pat on the back. For the protégé, however, the difference can be enormous. Just as there are preferred learning styles, so there may be communication techniques that are more desirable for an individual. The person who is more verbal will perceive the spoken word as true recognition. A physical touch—hug, handshake—has more affect on a person who is more kinesthetic. The written note will be appreciated by people whose inclinations are more visual.

Also, the mentor must balance the public versus private aspect of recognition. Mentors need to consider the school or system and the individual protégé when deciding which accomplishments should be acknowledged one-on-one and when they should be recognized before a group of peers, supervisors/administrators, or other staff members.

To provide meaningful recognition:

■ **Look for events and accomplishments worth celebrating.**

■ **Keep track of expressions of recognition so that there are no long periods without acknowledgment.**

■ **Observe the protégé's language to help determine preferred methods of communication. (Are there many references to seeing, to hearing/talking, or to touching?)**

■ **Carefully screen personal and organizational dynamics to create a balance between public and private acknowledgments.**

Developing the Mentoring Abilities of Others

Mentors are often viewed with awe by their protégés—and by others. Good mentors know not only when to encourage the protégé to be self-reliant, but they also know when and how to promote the role of mentor. Good mentors cultivate protégés who become fine educators, and they build a cadre of new mentors. The protégé needs to acquire the tools to be a mentor.

Achieving expertise in one's own job is not a sufficient base from which to become a mentor. A prospective mentor needs the knowledge and skill to perform well in a designated work role, but the person also needs to be willing and able to engage in the special tasks associated with mentoring. As a mentor develops mentoring potential in the protégé, it may be important for both to verbalize what has helped in the relationship—and what hasn't worked. It may be helpful to carefully look at the sequence of events. Of special significance may be the mentor's pattern(s) of behavior. Some aspects of successful mentoring are found in interpersonal characteristics and may be difficult to define. Other aspects are observable types of behavior that can and should be labeled and described.

To develop other people as mentors:

■ **Make a timeline using different colors of ink for the activities of mentor and protégé.**

■ **Generalize about the roles of mentor and protégé over time.**

■ **Make a list of questions about interpersonal characteristics.**

Redefining the Mentor's Role

Some aspects of serving as mentor are consistent with the norms of schools—it is generally regarded as desirable for educators to help and to teach. Other features seem to defy the way life in school really is—mentoring demands an openness and sharing that runs counter to the hoarding of ideas and materials that is often a byproduct of competition. As mentors and protégés work together, they redefine the mentor's role moment to moment, as well as over time, in ways that are mutually beneficial.

To be healthy, the mentoring relationship must remain balanced, whether conforming to the institutional culture or deviating from it. Mentor and protégé must strive to acknowledge the fit (or lack of fit) of what they are striving to achieve within the larger school picture. In addition, they must take care to keep the mentoring relationship itself healthy.

An outcome that should be healthy for mentor and protégé is increased confidence. Working with the protégé should make the mentor keenly aware of personal success. The opportunity to approach the job with guidance in avoiding common pitfalls should likewise bolster the protégé.

Further, as mentor and protégé work together, their communication skills should be enhanced. Each should be able to move quickly and to naturally "make sense" to the other. And both should be able to connect more easily with the larger environment within which they work.

Because the mentoring relationship is expected to change, trust is the key element. Each—mentor and protégé—must trust the confidentiality, the ability, the intent, and the commitment of the other. The mentor must redefine the mentoring role and be willing to "let go" without betraying or resenting the protégé. The protégé must acquire increased independence with dignity and without denying the importance of the mentor.

In forging a mutual relationship:

■ **Write or discuss the ways in which the mentoring relationship you wish to have runs counter to existing norms.**

■ **Design a "safety valve"—a signal that either mentor or protégé could use to indicate true difficulty within the relationship.**

■ **Verbally express appreciation for the benefits of the mentoring relationship.**

Reflecting on Oneself as Mentor

In ancient Corinth, the substance used to create mirrors produced only a dark, vague image of a person. Yet that image was deemed a reflection.

A still pool of water captures on its surface a likeness of the surrounding scenery or a person standing at its edge. And often that image is called a reflection. Great cities often have grand reflecting pools, such as the Reflecting Pool near the Washington Monument.

Modern mirrors give clear impressions; but as anyone who has tried to write by viewing hands in a mirror knows, there is a reversal. The reflection is not exact reality. In fact, children who see through mirror images (or write reversed letters) are often considered learning disabled.

Our experiences with reflection, both ancient and modern, remind us that reflection includes some changing of reality. As the mentor reflects on mentoring, the hard cold facts should be included. But the meaning attached to the mentoring experience will come through some new, personal insights that may give additional angles to the views, may use parts of available information, or may derive patterns as generalizations. In other words, there will be the kind of treatment of reality that we consider reflective.

A reflection on your role as mentor may include your own personal concept of mentoring. Have you, as a mentor, been a wise counselor, an avenue, a screen, a support, a role model? Insights should also relate to skills. To what extent have you been skillful in conducting the activities of mentoring? How are the skills being used? Where do you need increased proficiency? Are changes needed in areas related to assigned work roles, or are changes needed in mentoring abilities?

To reflect on mentoring:

■ **Look at the events of any given day to appreciate the good aspects and to determine what you would change if you could.**

■ **Keep a calendar of "high" and "low" points as a way of capturing the events and feelings of mentoring.**

■ **Take a longitudinal view of the mentoring to examine the ways in which the relationship has yielded benefits to the people involved and to education.**

As you reflect on what has happened, you should consider what you have avoided. Have you, as a mentor, resisted the temptation to make mentoring into something it should *not* be: a step-by-step process; a set of never-altered definable skills; one model; parenting?

Reflection should involve acceptance and acknowledgment of behavior that is conscious and represents competence. But don't sell yourself short as you review your experiences: often there are quantum leaps, internal or intuitive in nature, that lead to increased knowledge and action.

Ideas and Ideals

What are the boundaries for mentors?
How should mentors respond to cultural diversity?
What is the effect of mentoring on the mentor?

> *We shall not cease from*
> *exploration and the end of all*
> *our exploring will be to*
> *arrive where we started and*
> *know the place for the first time.*

—*T.S. Eliot,* **Four Quartets**

Getting and Keeping the Vision

Any person may be tempted to deal with fragments of the job to survive on a day-to-day basis. But survival will be insufficient in the long run for meeting the needs of people and institutions. *Having* and *reviewing* and *renewing* a vision are powerful antidotes to allowing the job to become custodial.

Vision is neither a record of reality nor seeing only what is visible to everyone else. Vision is the ability to see what could be as opposed to seeing only what is there. It may depend on looking outward and forward. Tom Peters (1987) reminds us that true leaders live their lives backwards: they look ahead to see where they wish to end up and adjust accordingly. But vision may also depend on the ability to look inward with new eyes.

As mentors work to get and keep the vision, they will focus on:

- Ability to generalize from the specific.
- Seeing the vision and participating in it.
- Being aware of ways in which their vision may represent a deviation from current institutional structure.
- Committing to the vision.
- Sharing the vision with others.

Mentors must be willing and able to maintain the vision independently; but it is equally critical that others understand the vision, so they can also follow it.

In the past, educators were often expected—even required—to lead separate personal and professional lives. This idea works as long as the topic is technically oriented. However, the real challenges and problems are not technical, but deal far more with the human spirit and basic human needs than with networks and computers and equipment. Therefore, part of getting the vision may be to ask mentors to bring their whole selves to

---

■ **Read to prime the pump. Read materials outside the field of education.**

■ **As you have ideas, write them down.**

■ **Listen carefully to other people's calls for actions and decisions as a way of understanding what is going on around you.**

---

their work, including to their mentoring. It may mean that in addition to heart and head, other aspects of the person—eyes, ears, mouth, and also seat of the pants—are part of the work.

For both mentors and protégés, energy, intuition, and consistent—if not constant—screening and critiquing will be required for getting and keeping vision in an environment of rapid change. No longer can one coast on previous experiences. Now mentoring must involve not only reflecting on and using one's past but also learning *with* the protégé in the present and keeping an orientation toward the future.

Focusing on Culture

American schools, theoretically available to all children and youths, historically have been most easily accessible to those who were white and middle class. Those in positions of leadership have fit a similar pattern; the majority of teachers have been white, middle class, and female.

The demographics of the United States are changing rapidly. Now, one American in four is Hispanic or nonwhite. Current trends point to an increase of 22 percent for Asian Americans, 21 percent for Hispanics, 12 percent for African Americans, and only 2 percent for whites by the beginning of the 21st century. The future pool of potential administrators is created by people who fit almost any description except the current one of white, middle class, and male.

The culture of schools and school administrations is not necessarily congruent with encouraging entry and growth by people from diverse backgrounds. The mentor's role in acknowledging, enjoying, and responding to cultural diversity may not be easy or immediate. Culture involves

> the dynamic interaction of attitudes, beliefs, behaviors, knowledge, ways of learning, customs, dress, environment, languages, and values of a group across its history (Hicks and Sullivan 1990).

Culture is not a surface phenomenon. Hunter Adams' (personal communication January 19, 1990) research indicates that, in fact, culture is neurologically embedded.

In seeking to be a mentor who revels in (not merely accepts) cultural diversity, one may start by increasing conscious awareness of one's own culture. Then one must look for the characteristics of others' cultures. Where are there contradictions to be resolved before other aspects of growing as a school administrator can take place?

■ **Make a personal poster or chart that captures your ideas about your own culture.**

■ **Ask a friend or colleague to alert you for examples of behavior or language that could be interpreted as biased against another culture.**

■ **Chart the projected demographic changes for your school or district and determine which cultures your educators will come from.**

Internalizing Skills

For experienced educators, many skills may have become automatic, part of their identity. Internalizing these skills may result in some cases from repetition. Often, it is also the product of awareness of what one is doing right.

Because mentoring requires more than the mechanistic exhibition of surface behavior, the skills associated with being a mentor, like other skills, should become intrinsic to the individual. Mentors need a clear notion of who they are and the way they mentor. In effect, internalizing skills contributes to a sense of steadiness about oneself.

Making mentoring second nature may require practice, observation, and study of one's own skills. It may require assessment and acknowledgement of one's natural ability. It may also call for risk-taking. Success in risky ventures leads to confidence.

As mentors internalize skills, they make the job look easy. That it comes smoothly and naturally does not mean it *is* easy, however.

■ **Chart your language pattern as a mentor. What words and phrases do you use often and successfully?**

■ **Determine the ways in which mentoring skills should remain constant for the mentor and the ways they should accommodate protégé needs.**

■ **Look ahead ten years. What should your résumé as mentor say? Plan your actions accordingly.**

Making a Plan for Mentoring

All of us know the story of the Edsel automobile.
Everybody thinks the Edsel failed because Ford didn't
do its homework. In fact, it was the best-engineered, the
best-researched, the best-everything car. There was
only one thing wrong with it: nobody in the Ford Motor
Company believed in it. It was contrived. It was
designed on the basis of research and not on the basis of
commitment. And so when it got into a little trouble,
nobody supported the child. I'm not saying it could
have been a success. But without that personal
commitment, it certainly never could be.

—*Peter Drucker,* **Managing the Nonprofit
Organization: Principles and Practices**
(1990, p. 7)

The following worksheets will enable educators to design customized plans. The worksheets include the opportunity to specify starting points, as well as focus on long-range growth that is both personal and professional in nature.

The divisions of the worksheets match the major sections of this text:

- Concepts of Mentoring
- Approaches
- Activities
- Ideas and Ideals

I.   What **concept of mentoring** will you emphasize?

_____

_____

_____

_____

_____

_____

_____

_____

_____

_____

_____

_____

_____

II.   Design your **approach**. List the components of formal and informal aspects you wish to use.

_____   _____

                               _____

_____   _____

                               _____

_____   _____

                               _____

_____   _____

                               _____

_____   _____

                               _____

_____   _____

                               _____

_____   _____

                               _____

III. List three **activities** to serve as your starting points.

_____

_____

_____

IV. Specify special targets—including **ideas and ideals**—to keep you
     focused on the future.

Vision _____

Culture _____

Internalizing _____

References

Barth, R. (May 1988). "Principals, Teachers and School Leadership." *Phi Delta Kappan* 69, 9: 640.

Coursen, D., J. Mazzarella, L. Jeffries, and M. Hadderman. (1989). *Two Special Cases: Women and Blacks.* Eugene, Ore.: Eric Clearinghouse on Educational Management.

Daniel, F.H. (August 1985). *Letting Go.* Sermon delivered at Decatur Presbyterian Church, Decatur, Georgia.

Darling-Hammond, L. (November 1988). "The Future of Teaching." *Educational Leadership* 46, 3: 4–10.

Drucker, P. (1990). *Managing the Nonprofit Organization: Principles and Practices.* New York: Harper Collins.

Edmonds, R. (October 1979). "Effective Schools for the Urban Poor." *Educational Leadership* 37: 15–24.

Eisner, E. (March 1990). Keynote address. ASCD Annual Conference, San Antonio.

Glasser, W. (1986). *Control Theory in the Classroom.* New York: Harper and Row.

Glickman, C.D. (1985). *Supervision of Instruction: A Developmental Approach.* Boston: Allyn and Bacon.

Gray, W. (Winter 1989). "Situational Mentoring: Custom Designing Planned Mentoring Programs." *Mentoring International* 3: 19.

Gray, W.A., and M.M. Gray. (November 1985). "Synthesis of Research on Mentoring Beginning Teachers." *Educational Leadership* 43, 3: 37–43.

Louis Harris & Associates. (1988). *The Metropolitan Life Survey of American Teachers: Strengthening the Relationship Between Teachers and Students.* New York: Metropolitan Life Insurance Company.

Hicks, B., and C. Sullivan. (1990). *Cross-Cultural Connection Training Manual.* Atlanta: Southeast Consortium for Minorities in Engineering.

Jensen, M.C. (1987). *How to Recruit, Select, Induct and Retain the Very Best Teachers.* Eugene, Ore.: Eric Clearinghouse on Educational Management.

Klauss, R. (1981). "Formalized Mentor Relationships for Management and Executive Development Programs in the Federal Government." *Public Administrative Review* 41, 1 : 489–496.

Levinson, D.J. (1978). *The Seasons of a Man's Life*. New York: Ballantine Books.

Little, J.W. (1990). "The Mentor Phenomenon and the Social Organization of Teaching." In *Review of Research in Education* (pp. 297–352), edited by C.T. Casden. Washington, D.C.: American Education Research Association.

Pence, L.J. (1989). "Mentorship Programs for Aspiring and New School Administrators." *OSSC Bulletin Series* 32, 7: 3–34. Eugene: Oregon School Study Council, University of Oregon.

Peters, T. (1987). *Thriving on Chaos: Handbook for a Management Revolution*. New York: Alfred Knopf.

Robbins, P. (1991). *How to Plan and Implement a Peer Coaching Program*. Alexandria, Va.: ASCD.

Shulman, L. (March 1991). Address presented at the ASCD Annual Conference, San Francisco.

Sullivan, C.G., and M.S. Murray. (1988). *Summary Report on Douglas County Teacher to Teacher Program*. Douglasville, Ga.: Douglasville County Schools.